KITTENS

CHECKERBOARD PRESS ◆ NEW YORK

I wonder what
all the fuss
is about . . .
haven't they
ever seen
a folding chair
before?

Look,
there's a new kitty.
What beautiful brown
eyes she has!

Yes, and such
fluffy brown fur!

Please come and
pull our wagon.
We want to go
for a ride.

We kittens
mee-ow and scamper
about and blink
our eyes.
But Bear just sits
and won't play
with us.

Oh, dear! Oh, dear!
Has anyone seen
our baby kitten?

We have;
she's right there
on the grass.

This basket isn't big enough to hold five kitties. Can't you see that we need more room?

Flowers are so pretty to look at. Which color do you like best?

I love trinkets and beads. Ah, a long chain of pearls... let's play.

Okay, we're ready!

What do you think these kittens are looking at? It may be a little sparrow. Or is it a big, fat robin?

Holly and mistletoe — Christmas will soon be here!

Don't you wish
that you had
a nice swing like ours?
If you give us a push,
then we'll give
you a ride.

Copyright © 1983 Colour Library Books Ltd.
Text copyright © 1984 Checkerboard Press, a division of Macmillan, Inc.
All rights reserved. Printed in U.S.A.

CHECKERBOARD PRESS Colophon are trademarks of Macmillan, Inc.